DEDICATION

THIS BOOK IS DEDICATED TO AMY FOR SUPPORTING ME THROUGH ONE OF THE HARDEST CHAPTERS OF MY LIFE.

'NO'
YOU CAN ALWAYS *SAY*
<u>NO</u>.

"No, I don't like that"

NO TICKLES PLEASE.

NO, I DON'T LIKE CHEESE.

"No thank you"

I AM NOT HERE TO APPEASE.

...IS WHAT I WILL SAY!
IT'S OKAY
IF YOU DON'T LIKE IT THAT WAY.
BUT THAT'S WHAT MY BODY
BOUNDARIES ARE TODAY.

'NO!'

IS THE ANSWER, I HAVE MADE UP MY MIND.

MY BODY, MY CHOICE IS WHAT I SAY.
THAT IS MY CHOICE FOR TODAY.

"GIVE ME A HUG" I WILL NOT OBEY.

SO, IF I SAY "NO"
PLEASE RESPECT ME SO.
JUST LIKE MR. JOE, WHEN I SAY NO.

THESE ARE MY BODY BOUNDARIES.
THEY ARE HERE TO STAY.
SO, PLEASE LISTEN TO WHAT I HAVE TO SAY.

www.ingramcontent.com/pod-product-compliance
Lightning Source LLC
Chambersburg PA
CBHW042053030526
44107CB00090B/1558